Bow Hunting

By Aileen Weintraub

Consultant:
Marilyn Bentz
Executive Director
National Bowhunter Education Foundation
Fort Smith, Arkansas

Capstone
press

Mankato, Minnesota

Capstone High-Interest Books are published by Capstone Press
151 Good Counsel Drive, P.O. Box 669, Mankato, Minnesota 56002
www.capstonepress.com

Library of Congress Cataloging-in-Publication Data
Weintraub, Aileen, 1973–
    Bow Hunting/by Aileen Weintraub
    p. cm.—(The great outdoors)
    Includes bibliographical references and index (p. 48).
    ISBN 0-7368-2410-3 (hardcover)
    1. Bow hunting—Juvenile literature. [1. Bow Hunting. 2. Hunting.]
I. Title. II. Series
SK36 .W45 2004
799.2'15—dc22   2003018352

Summary: Discusses the history, needed equipment, and techniques of hunting
with a bow and arrow, as well as related safety and conservation issues.

Editorial Credits
James Anderson, editor; Timothy Halldin, series designer; Molly Nei, book
    designer and illustrator; Jo Miller, photo researcher

Photo Credits
Bill Marchel, cover (top)
Bruce Coleman Inc./Larry R. Ditto, 4
Capstone Press/Gary Sundermeyer, cover (bottom, inset), 13, 14, 17, 21, 25, 26, 29, 36, 39
Comstock, 1
Corbis/AFP, 9; D. Robert & Lorri Franz, 42 (top); Geoffrey Clements, 7; Lowell
Georgia, 30; Royalty-Free, 40
Corel, 18, 42 (bottom), 43 (all)
Eyewire Images, 34
Leonard Rue Enterprises, 10, 33
Wade Nolan, AWP, Inc., 22

1 2 3 4 5 6 09 08 07 06 05 04

Table of Contents

CHAPTER 1

Bow Hunting

People have hunted for food since prehistoric times. Hunting has also been a way of getting fur and leather for clothing. Today, most people no longer have to hunt to survive. But hunting is still popular. People hunt because it is fun and challenging.

Bow hunting dates back thousands of years. Ancient Egyptians were among the earliest known people to use a bow and arrow to hunt for food. Bows and arrows were also used as weapons.

Later in history, using a bow became a sport. The sport is called archery. In China, people took part in archery games. Archery contests were also popular in England.

Bow hunters enjoy the challenge of hunting with a bow and arrows.

Archery continued to be a popular sport in England for many years. It was mainly a sport for wealthy people. Bow hunting became known as the "sport of kings."

American Indian Bow Hunters

Some American Indian groups hunted with bows and arrows. American Indians had traditional ways of making bows and arrows. Some used the Osage orange tree to make their bows. This tree has thick, strong limbs. The limbs bend easily without breaking. The hickory tree was used for making arrows.

Some American Indians used tendons from deer or other large animals as string for their bows. Indians cut the tendons into short strands. They then tied the strands together to fit the bow.

Some arrows were made from bison, deer, and other animal bones. American Indians also used river cane to make arrows. This tall, thin plant is completely straight, but not as strong as animal bones.

Some American Indians used bows and arrows to hunt bison.

Bow Hunting in the United States

The United Bowmen of Philadelphia was the first organized bow hunting group in the United States. The group lasted from 1828 to 1859. In 1879, the National Archery Association formed. This group still exists today.

Saxton Pope and Arthur Young are often called the fathers of modern bow hunting. In the early 1900s, they met an American Indian named Ishi. He taught them how to bow hunt.

Aldo Leopold was another early U.S. bow hunter. Leopold helped to make bow hunting a sport. He was concerned for animals and the environment. Leopold created a hunting season for hunters who use a bow and arrows. This season was separate from rifle hunting season. Many states now have bow hunting seasons.

Today, about 3 million people hunt with bows and arrows. Some of these hunters feel closer to nature because they are hunting the way early people did. Bow hunters believe that hunting with a bow and arrow is a challenging sport that takes patience.

Because of the early growth of archery, the sport is now a part of the Olympic Games. Women and men from around the world compete in various events of skill using bows and arrows.

Archers from around the world compete in the Olympic Games.

CHAPTER 2

Equipment

Bows and arrows can be made of different materials. Most modern bows are made of wood or metal. Most arrows are made of aluminum or carbon fiber. Wood arrows are sometimes used by archers who enjoy using traditional equipment. Some wood arrows are made of cedar.

Arrows

The shaft is the middle of the arrow. Bow hunters call an arrow's shaft its "spine." It is a long tube that connects the tip to the fletchings. Fletchings are feathers or plastic vanes at one end of the arrow. The spine of an arrow determines how stiff it is. An arrow with a stiff spine does not bend easily.

Bow hunters use arrows that do not bend easily.

Fletchings keep an arrow steady while it flies. They can be 3, 4, or 5 inches (8, 10, or 13 centimeters) long. Fletchings can be made of feathers or plastic. Feathers are lighter than plastic vanes when they are dry. But plastic vanes will not absorb water when it rains. Bow hunters use dry, lightweight arrows.

The plastic notch at the back end of an arrow is called a nock. The nock is used to hold the arrow in place on the bowstring. As soon as the hunter lets go of the string, the arrow shoots forward. Without the nock, an arrow would fall to the ground when the archer pulled back the string.

Hunters use different types of tips on their arrows. Blunts are tips that are not sharp or pointed. They can be used to hunt small animals. Broadheads are sharp arrow tips with blades. They are used for hunting large animals.

Arrow Styles

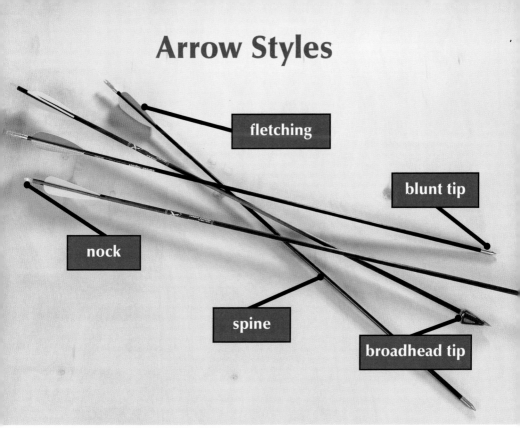

fletching

blunt tip

nock

spine

broadhead tip

Bow Styles

Bow hunters use three types of bows.
They are the compound bow, the longbow,
and the recurve bow. These bows look
different from each other. But they have
similar features. Each bow has a handle,
a string, and limbs.

Bow Styles

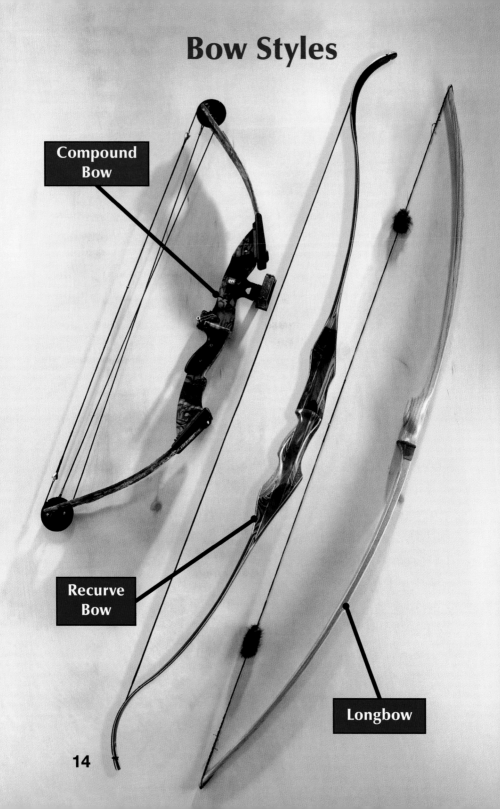

Compound Bow

Recurve Bow

Longbow

Hunters have to hold the bowstring back for a long time. Compound bows have cams. These round or oval wheels are on the top and bottom of the bow. They release tension and make it easier for hunters to hold the string while it is pulled back.

Recurve bows look different from compound bows. Recurve bows' limbs are bent forward, away from the hunter. Recurve bows are thick at the center. Hunters grip this area when they pull the bowstring.

Longbows look similar to recurve bows. They have narrow limbs and thick grip areas. Longbows are lightweight. Bow makers often carve longbows from one piece of wood.

Bow Accessories

Bow hunters place kissers on the bowstring. Hunters use kissers to make sure the bow is pulled the same way every time. When the bowstring is pulled back, the kisser should touch the hunter's lips. If it touches the same place every time, the bow hunter will be more likely to shoot accurately each time.

Many bow hunters use a release when they bow hunt. Bow hunters use the release to pull the string back. A release helps the hunter shoot accurately. Most releases wrap around the hunter's wrist and attach to the bowstring. Hunters do not hurt their fingers on the string when they use a release. The arrow shoots when a bow hunter lets go of a trigger on the release.

A quiver attaches to the bow and holds arrows. Some quivers can also be worn on the hip or over the shoulder. Bow hunters can easily reach into their quivers to get more arrows.

Taking Care of a Bow

Hunters must take care of their bows to keep them in good condition. The strings and cables need to be waxed often. Bow hunters apply bowstring wax to keep the bowstring from being damaged by water.

Bow hunters check their bow for damage before using it. They make sure the string is not frayed.

A bow hunter uses a release to hold the bowstring.

Hunters check for cracks by rubbing a cotton ball along the wood. If there are cracks, the cotton will get caught in the bow. Hunters bring cracked bows to hunting specialty shops to have them repaired.

Clothing

Hunters wear specific clothing while hunting. They wear clothing that does not brush together and make noise when they move. Even a small noise can scare an animal away.

Hunters' clothing should be warm in cold weather. Hunters wear extra layers when the temperature is cool. Fleece is a warm material that many hunters wear. Hunters wear hats, coats, gloves, and wool socks in cold weather.

Many hunters wear camouflage clothing. These clothes are dyed with colors that blend with the colors of trees, grass, and snow. Camouflage clothing makes it harder for animals to see hunters.

Many states have laws about the colors of clothing that hunters wear. Some state laws say that all hunters need to wear bright orange clothing in the woods. Bright orange clothing allows hunters to see each other and not mistake hunters for animals.

Some bow hunters wear clothing that blends with their surroundings.

Other Equipment

Hunters carry a variety of equipment. All hunters should carry first aid kits. Hunters should also carry a compass to find their way in the outdoors. Most hunters carry binoculars to help them see their targets. Large binoculars are used to see targets at a distance.

Hunters always carry a hunting knife. They use knives to clean out certain internal organs from an animal after it has been killed. These organs could spoil the meat if they are left in the animal's body.

Hunters carry products that hide their scent. Deer have a very good sense of smell. Some hunters hide their scent by rubbing branches from cedar trees on themselves.

Bow hunters may add a stabilizer to a bow. A stabilizer reduces noise and vibrations as an arrow is shot. Stabilizers allow bow hunters to shoot their arrows long distances.

Some bow hunters also wear an arm guard. The arm guard protects a hunter's forearm from being scraped by the bowstring.

compound bow

jacket

pants

arrows

recurve bow

treestand

hat

call bag

safety harness

arm guard

small binoculars

binoculars

Equipment

- arm guard
- arrows
- binoculars
- call bag
- camouflage pants and jacket
- compound bow
- hat
- recurve bow
- safety harness
- small binoculars
- treestand

21

Skills and Techniques

M any bow hunters have favorite techniques they use to get close to their prey. Hunters want to make sure that they have the best chance of hitting the animal they are hunting.

Treestands

Treestands are raised platforms attached to a tree. Hunters sit in treestands while looking for prey. Animals are less likely to see hunters in a treestand.

Hunters need to know how to use a treestand safely. They practice shooting their bow from a raised position before using a treestand in the woods. They also must wear a safety harness.

A hunter in a treestand wears a safety harness.

Most hunters use portable treestands that they bring with them when they enter the woods. These portable stands allow hunters to move from one tree to another.

Rattling

Hunters use different ways to attract the attention of an animal or get a deer to pass closely by. Rattling is one technique that hunters use to call bucks, or male deer. A hunter may use old antlers from a deer or antlers made of plastic.

The hunter takes one set of antlers in each hand and clicks them together. This rattling sound is like two bucks fighting. The sound attracts other bucks to the area.

Calling

Hunters often make sounds to attract animals. A hunter might make a grunting noise. If the noise is similar to the sound that deer make, the hunter may attract deer.

Bow hunters click antlers together to attract deer.

A hunter may also blow into a tube to attract animals. The tubes are called "calls." When a person blows into a call, a sound is produced. Calls are made that sound like deer, turkeys, bears, and other animals.

Hunters try to be still and quiet while stalking.

Stalking

Hunters walk through the woods looking for deer or other animals to stalk. They walk very slowly and try to be as quiet as possible.

Stalking is a difficult hunting technique. Most animals can hear very well. Even though hunters think they are being quiet, they may make sounds that only animals can hear. Animals often run away from hunters who are stalking.

Decoys

A bow hunter looking for wild turkey, deer, antelope, or elk may set up decoys. These wood or plastic animals look like real animals. Bow hunters have a better shot at animals that are still. A deer that sees a decoy will often approach it and stand still by the decoy.

Blinds

Many hunters use different types of blinds. Blinds help hide hunters. Some hills, trees, and brush are natural blinds. Bow hunters hide behind these objects. Hunters may also cover themselves with leaves and branches.

Many hunters carry portable blinds with them when they hunt. Hunters can buy blinds. These blinds may include a small shelter or a wall painted camouflage colors. Hunters often set up blinds near an area where animals go to eat.

Hunters try their blinds at different locations. If no animals approach the blind, the hunter may move the blind to another hunting site.

Some hunters check for sites before they hunt. They watch for deer, bear, or turkey. They then set up their blind the night before they go hunting.

Country Style Venison Stew

Ingredients:

½ pound (225 grams) bacon
2 pounds (910 grams) venison steak
4 tablespoons (60 mL) flour
6 cups (1,440 mL) water or beef broth
1 large tomato, chopped
2 medium carrots, sliced
2 medium stalks celery, sliced
2 medium potatoes, cut into 1-inch
   (2.5-centimeter) cubes
12 small white onions

1 tablespoon (15 mL) chopped
   parsley
1 cup (240 mL) fresh green peas
salt and pepper

Equipment:
knife
large saucepan
spoon
liquid measuring cup
pan
strainer

What You Do:

1. Cut bacon into 1-inch (2.5-centimeter) cubes and cook in large saucepan until lightly browned. Remove bacon and set aside.
2. Cut venison into 2-inch (5-centimeter) pieces and brown over high heat in bacon drippings.
3. Stir in flour. Lower heat and let brown 2–3 minutes, stirring several times.
4. Add water or beef broth and simmer 1 hour or more until venison begins to get tender. Add more liquid as necessary.
5. Add all the other ingredients, except peas, and continue to simmer to make a thick stew.
6. Simmer peas in a separate pan until done. Drain and spoon over or around stew when served.

Serves: 4   *Children should have adult supervision.*

HEADQUARTERS

NATIONAL
BISON RANGE

ESTABLISHED 1908 WITH AID OF
AMERICAN BISON SOCIETY

30

CHAPTER 4

Conservation

In the early 1800s, millions of bison lived in the United States. By the end of that century, there were only 400 bison left. Hunters had killed too many bison. Deer and bighorn sheep were also overhunted. These animals were in danger of dying out because there were no laws to protect them.

Bow hunters help protect animals. They obey laws and work to keep the outdoors clean and free of pollution.

Hunting Laws

Today's hunting laws help to protect animals from being overhunted. One law states that there has to be a hunting season. Hunting is only allowed during this time. Bow hunting season occurs between September and November in most states.

Several national programs protect endangered animals.

Some laws determine the kind or number of animals a hunter can shoot. A law may say that deer hunters can only shoot one buck and up to three does, or female deer, per season.

Other laws say what time of day hunters can hunt. Most states do not allow bow hunting before daylight or after dark. Hunters cannot see well in the woods at night. A person who hunts when it is dark may accidentally shoot an animal that should not be hunted.

Other laws protect endangered animals. Hunters cannot kill an animal whose population is in danger of dying out. Hunters should know which animals are endangered. Hunters who kill endangered animals can be sent to jail or never be allowed to hunt again.

Keeping the Outdoors Clean

The outdoors is a place for all people to enjoy. People who spend time outdoors should respect the environment.

Bow hunters are only allowed to shoot a certain number of bucks or does each season.

Conservation programs protect young animals from being hunted.

Hunters should clean up after themselves. They should follow the "leave no trace" rule. When they are leaving the woods, the area should look like the hunters have never been there.

Wildlife Conservation

Many groups in the United States are involved in protecting wildlife. Some of these groups include the U.S. Fish and Wildlife Service and the National Audubon Society. These groups teach people about wildlife conservation. They also plan conservation programs that offer safe areas for young and endangered animals to live.

National parks are also involved in wildlife conservation. They were created to protect wildlife and their habitats. People are not allowed to hunt in national parks. Many animals that are hard to find elsewhere can be seen in national parks.

Each state has wildlife conservation programs. The fees that states collect for hunting licenses often pay for activities that protect land and wildlife. Some states have extra taxes on hunting equipment. Money from these taxes is also used to preserve land and animals.

CHAPTER 5

Safety

Bow hunting can be dangerous. Bow hunters must know and follow safety rules. Bow hunters also need to know how to use hunting equipment safely.

Treestand Safety

Hunters check their treestands for damage before putting them in a tree. They also check the tree where the stand will be placed. They make sure that the stand will not damage the tree. They also check to see if the tree is strong enough to hold the hunter.

Hunters wear safety harnesses while in a treestand. The harness is attached to the tree above the treestand. If hunters slip, the harness stops them from falling below the treestand.

Bow hunters check their treestand before climbing.

Hunters do not climb trees while holding their bow and arrows. If they fall, they could land on an arrow. Hunters climb to the treestand first. They use ropes called hauling lines to pull up their equipment once they are already in the tree.

Being Responsible with Arrows

Bow hunters check their arrows before shooting. A damaged arrow can be dangerous. A broken arrow could snap back when the string is pulled.

Hunters make sure a target can be seen before shooting. If an arrow is carelessly shot into the air, it could come back down and hit the hunter or someone else.

Hunters should never point an arrow at a target that they do not want to shoot. Hunters need to be aware of what might be behind their target. They should not shoot if they are not sure of what the arrow could strike if they miss.

A bow hunter uses a hauling line to lift and lower a bow and arrows to the treestand.

Many scouting groups teach basic archery skills.

Safety Training

Bow hunters need safety training before they hunt. Many experienced bow hunters take courses to learn about new hunting laws. Scouting groups offer many bow hunting and archery courses.

Many hunting laws are taught in bow hunting safety classes. Hunters have to obey these laws as well as use good technique.

All states offer bow hunting safety courses. In many states, a bow hunter must complete a safety course before applying for a license.

Some states have a minimum age requirement for a person requesting a bow hunting license. Most states say that a hunter must be 14 years old. Young bow hunters should check with wildlife agencies in their state to learn about hunting safety courses.

Good hunters have both hunting skills and safety knowledge. These hunters know that proper equipment and safety are important for hunters, animals, and the environment. Good bow hunters come prepared for their adventures in the outdoors.

Mule Deer

Description: Mule deer are gray-brown in color. They have a narrow white tail with a black tip. Some mule deer have a white patch on their throat or chin. Mule deer are known for their large, fuzzy ears. A male mule deer can weigh up to 400 pounds (181 kilograms). A female may weigh up to 200 pounds (91 kilograms).
Habitat: woods, grassy areas, mountains, river valleys
Food: grasses, leaves

White-tailed Deer

Description: White-tailed deer are red-brown. Their tails are brown and white. The underside of the tail is completely white. These deer also have white patches on their nose, throat, and around their eyes. A male white-tail can weigh up to 300 pounds (136 kilograms). A female can weigh up to 200 pounds (91 kilograms).
Habitat: woods, grassy areas
Food: grasses, leaves

American Black Bear

Description: Some American black bears are not completely black. Some are brown, and some have white patches on their chest. Black bears can run up to 25 miles (40 kilometers) per hour. They can grow to be 5 feet (1.5 meters) long and weigh between 200 to 500 pounds (91 to 227 kilograms).

Habitat: forests in northern United States, Canada

Food: mice, squirrels, fish, bird eggs, berries, fruit, nuts, leaves, roots

Wild Turkey

Description: Wild turkeys have long legs and a long neck. They have dark feathers. They also have very small heads. Males have bronze-colored feathers. Female turkeys have light brown feather tips on the front part of their body. A male turkey can weigh up to 16 pounds (7 kilograms). A female turkey averages about 9 pounds (4 kilograms).

Habitat: forests, wooded and grassy areas

Food: insects, seeds, small nuts, fruits

43

Glossary

aluminum (uh-LOO-mi-nuhm)—a lightweight, silver-colored metal

archery (AR-chuh-ree)—the sport of shooting at targets using a bow and arrow

camouflage (KAM-uh-flahzh)—clothing that makes hunters blend in with their surroundings

carbon (KAR-buhn)—strong, lightweight fibers sometimes used to make arrows

environment (en-VYE-ruhn-muhnt)—the natural world of the land and animals

prehistoric (pree-hi-STOR-ik)—from a time before history was recorded

technique (tek-NEEK)—a way of doing something that requires skill

Read More

Ceasar, Jonathan. *Essential Deer Hunting for Teens*. Outdoor Life. New York: Children's Press, 2000.

Frahm, Randy. *Deer Hunting*. The Great Outdoors. Mankato, Minn.: Capstone Press, 2002.

Useful Addresses

Canadian Wildlife Federation
350 Michael Cowpland Drive
Kanata, ON K2M 2W1
Canada

National Archery Association
One Olympic Plaza
Colorado Springs, CO 80909

U.S. Fish and Wildlife Service
4401 North Fairfax Drive
Arlington, VA 22203

Internet Sites

FactHound offers a safe, fun way to find Internet sites related to this book. All of the sites on FactHound have been researched by our staff.

Here's how:
1. Visit *www.facthound.com*
2. Type in this special code **0736824103** for age-appropriate sites. Or enter a search word related to this book for a more general search.
3. Click on the **Fetch It** button.

FactHound will fetch the best sites for you!

Index